A souvenir guide

Baddesley Clinton

Warwickshire

G000166772

☘ National Trust

A Romantic Retreat

A house and garden deeply imbued with a historic atmosphere, at one time a haven for the persecuted, at another an artists' retreat, Baddesley Clinton is both intriguing and romantic, and deserves a much closer look.

If we had been visitors to Baddesley Clinton in the 1870s, we would have encountered a picturesque moated manor house, looking much as it does today. The gardens were a bit fuller and more ornamental, and there would have been more than a modest hum of servant activity in both house and stables. We might well have also met or glimpsed the equally picturesque inhabitants.

A squire in the old style

The best-known 19th-century squire of Baddesley Clinton was Marmion Ferrers (1813–84), the 12th generation of the Ferrers family to have lived here. He adored his family home and all its antiquity. He even used to dress the part in a Charles the First-style hat, velvet breeches and jacket, and sported a pointed beard. In a way, he 'wore the house' and with the prevailing 19th-century Romanticism for the past, people regarded him as a living embodiment of old English ways. He was a squire in the old-fashioned style, and was widely thought of as a man of duty, a benign leader of a little agricultural community, who looked back to the days when the lord of the manor oversaw the estate and its workers (see next chapter). He was the representative of a world remote from the modernising industry of Birmingham, a little over a dozen miles away.

Origins of Baddesley
The name Baddesley has Saxon origins and is thought to refer to a Saxon called Badde, who had a clearing in the wood here within the ancient Forest of Arden, hence the name Badde's ley. A manor is known to have existed here at the time of the Norman Conquest in 1066, one of the many granted to the Norman knight, Geoffrey de Wirce. It was granted later to Nigel d'Albini, whose son bestowed it on Walter de Bisege. Bisege's great-granddaughter, Mazera, then married Sir Thomas de Clinton. Sir Thomas, or his son James, is thought to have dug the moat, and changed the name of the manor to Baddesley Clinton. The manor remained in the hands of the de Clintons for another four generations.

Right Marmion Ferrers liked to play the part of a squire from an earlier time

Opposite Baddesley Clinton romantically depicted by one of its artistic residents, Rebecca Dulcibella Orpen, later Rebecca Ferrers, 1898

Marmion shares his passion

Marmion's enthusiasm for the old English ways was something he shared with his wife, and this way of life gained followers when practical needs and a lack of resources led to the arrival of two new residents with similarly old-fashioned views.

Marmion's artistic dress was probably encouraged by his wife Rebecca (1830–1923), 17 years his junior, whom he married in 1867. She was a talented and prolific painter, who not

Left An early self-portrait of Rebecca, then aged 26, 1856

Below left Georgiana, Lady Chatterton (1806–76)

Below right Lady Chatterton's second husband, Edward Dering (1827–92)

Artistic types

The Derings moved in artistic circles. Both were novelists and Lady Chatterton had known Bulwer Lytton, Dickens and Wordsworth. For many artistic people of the 19th century, as the restless expansion of industry and urbanisation was changing the face of England, the very idea of the old English moated manor house, steeped in history with a small community run in some ways like a large family, held considerable appeal.

Keeping the faith

For Rebecca and the Derings, Baddesley Clinton was also associated with Roman Catholicism. All three were 'received' in 1865 into the Roman Catholic church by John Newman (later Cardinal Newman). The Ferrers family had remained Catholics since the Reformation, which to the imagination of a 19th-century Romantic added an almost irresistible lustre to the family's ancient lineage.

As the *Birmingham Daily Gazette* put it in November 1892: 'Baddesley Clinton Hall … is one of the "show places" of Warwickshire. It has a somewhat unique history. It has been in the possession of the Ferrers family for nearly 500 years, and during the whole of that long period has never been owned by a Protestant master. The Ferrerses have remained true to the ancient Catholic faith through the long line of their descent, and through centuries of trouble and trial.'

Watercolours from visits to various country estates by Lady Chatterton and Rebecca

Left Castle Mahon near Cork, the seat of Sir James Chatterton Bt, by Lady Chatterton, 1824–48

Below An interior of a stately home visited and painted by Rebecca, 1840–70

only filled the house with family portraits but also painted many views of Baddesley Clinton.

Despite his impressive family tree (see inside back cover) and his mother being the daughter of an earl, Marmion, the charming, sporting squire, was never well off. For this reason, in 1869 Rebecca's aunt, Georgiana, Lady Chatterton (the widow of Irish landowner Sir William Chatterton) and her aunt's second husband, Edward Dering, came to live with them. Marmion and Edward used to joke about how their ancestors had fought on opposing sides at the Battle of Hastings: the Ferrers family was descended from a Norman knight who had crossed with William the Conqueror; the Derings traced their lineage to Saxon landowners.

The love of Old England

Edward poured a considerable amount of his own money into Baddesley Clinton, to prevent Marmion and Rebecca having to sell their beloved home, which also seemed to symbolise to him the best of old England. They all knew old England rather well, as Lady Chatterton, Edward and Rebecca were enthusiastic country house visitors. Rebecca filled albums with watercolours of the houses where they stayed, many of which were grand classical 18th-century piles, others 19th-century Gothic fantasies.

The Quartet is formed

All four – Marmion, Rebecca, Lady Chatterton and Edward Dering – were in love with an ideal, but this had real, practical consequences. Baddesley Clinton for them held a charm that they all sought to preserve, and it rewarded their efforts by fulfilling their romantic notions and providing them with a harmonious home.

Together they restored and refurnished the house, re-created the Chapel (see page 51) and extended the servants' wing (designed by Edward who also supervised its building), which merges into the old manor house surprisingly well. They must have seemed eccentric to the outside world, dressed in their old-fashioned clothes, living out their dreams in a draughty old manor house, but they drew admiration as well as curiosity, and the two inseparable couples became known as the Quartet.

A poetic life

The Quartet lived what one writer in the 1930s called a 'gentle Tennysonian existence', and reflected something of the 19th-century revival of ideals of chivalry and courtly love. (Alfred, Lord Tennyson [1809–92] was Poet Laureate for much of the Victorian age and his writings celebrated these themes.) After Marmion's death, his mantle of squire of the manor passed to Edward. Lady Chatterton had died in 1876, so a year after Marmion's death, the Quartet now a duet, Edward married Rebecca,

There was considerable anxiety that such a house would be lost. However, the same nostalgic tug for the old stone manor house that had inspired the Quartet moved others to intervene. It was acquired first by a philanthropist, Coker Iliffe, and later by a distant relative of the Ferrers family, Thomas Walker (1888–1970) and his wife Undine (1894–1962). In demonstration of their commitment to the place, they even changed their name to Ferrers-Walker and then to Ferrers.

They were followed by their son, Thomas Weaving Ferrers-Walker (1925–2006), who handed the house over to the National Trust in 1980, with generous endowments from two members of the Mellor family (the sister and niece of Graham, Baron Ash of Packwood). The National Trust opened Baddesley Clinton to the public in 1982. Since then, those who work for the National Trust and many locally based volunteers have carried the torch for this remarkable place into the 21st century.

Opposite *Self-portrait, The Artist At Her Easel* by Rebecca, 1885

Left A portrait of Lady Chatterton by Rebecca, 1850–76

Below A double portrait of Edward Dering by Rebecca, 1850–84

who had inherited a life interest in the house, which Edward had helped save. Indeed in 1890 he paid off much of the existing mortgages and debts. After Edward died in 1892, Rebecca lived out her second widowhood with the company of a few devoted servants until her death in 1923.

A new world

When Rebecca died, the money was again running out, and Marmion's nephews could not keep the place going, although it still looks romantic enough in the photographs taken for *Country Life* in 1932. In 1939, the estate was put up for sale by the family's trustees, and furniture, which had not already been sold during the 1930s, was sold at auction in 1940.

The spirit of the place lives on

In many ways, the house has changed little from the days of the Quartet, and the great majority of the paintings you see hanging on the walls were painted by Rebecca, including copies of old family portraits which had been lost or passed to other branches of the family.

Before Lady Chatterton and Edward Dering came to live with Marmion and Rebecca, the house appears to have been sparsely furnished and to have had few pictures. Rebecca's paintings and late 19th-century photographs capture a mellow, old oak interior, in which armorial stained glass, carved chimneypieces and tapestries played an important role. The house would have smelt of wood fires, polish, candlewax and cut flowers from the garden.

A retreat from the modern world

Baddesley Clinton was for Marmion and his friends, and for the many Roman Catholic priests they entertained here, a haven from the modern world, a spiritual retreat. The writer Fletcher Moss visited during Rebecca's widowhood and revelled in the dappled light of the stained glass, the 'oaken panelled walls … almost hidden by works of art…. The drowsy air of a summer afternoon is redolent of roses. The waters of the moat are lapping on the walls below the open window.' He also wrote of Rebecca: 'In thorough harmony with the place is the Lady of the Manor, a handsome courteous elderly lady whose time is spent in works of charity, and who comes to say a few words of welcome not only for this day but also for another.'

Above Baddesley Clinton is little changed since the days of the Quartet

Opposite left *The Squire's Evening Walk*; Marmion Edward Ferrers painted by Rebecca, 1870

Opposite right *The Philosopher's Morning Walk*; Edward Dering painted by Rebecca, 1867–92

The painter's eye

Rebecca's paintings hang throughout the house. Of particular interest are the 1870 view of the Great Hall with the Quartet at leisurely repose (see page 46), and also the soulful 1885 self-portrait, which shows her standing in the Great Parlour, in mourning dress, beside an easel with a painting of the old manor house (page 6). In some ways, Rebecca is still on hand to welcome us today, through the many paintings in the house that vividly capture the sense of how much the Quartet enjoyed living in these intimate old rooms.

An antiquarian's view

In *Pilgrimages to Old Homes* (1912), Fletcher Moss recalled being greeted at the door by a priest in Benedictine dress, and also a manservant being present in one room with Rebecca. 'In the quaint epauletted livery of black is a butler whose mien is that of a family servant – not one who is bought with mere wages, but a survival from the days when servants were serfs or chattels, bred and reared on, and part of, the estate.'

Life in the Manor

A medieval manor was a complex social unit with a lord of the manor holding all the power and peasants working the land for their lord as well as for themselves. This community, born of necessity, became a model for successful communal living.

A manor house was the principal residence of the lord of the manor or his representative, the steward or bailiff. From the early Middle Ages, the manor house was usually centred on an open hall. This provided a social space and was also where local disputes were heard. The hall had a platform, or dais, at one end, where the lord and his family and guests would sit, with the rest of the household on long tables at ground level. A stair at the dais end of the hall usually led to a first-floor great chamber, the more intimate preserve of the lord and his family. A kitchen and pantry (for bread) and buttery (for wine and ale) lay at the other end of the hall, the entrance passage between the two concealed by a screen. This is the classic architectural pattern of the English manor.

Working the land

From Norman times, the manor would have its own demesne, or land which the lord farmed, while the rest was divided into strips (selions) farmed by the peasants. Many villages were made up of two or three manors, although in others all the villagers might be the tenants of a single lord. In the Norman period, the most numerous peasants were the serfs, bound to the lord of the manor for life, who held land in return for service, effectively rents in kind.

The parallel strips or selions were separated by raised banks of unploughed land. Physical evidence of this medieval strip farming, or ridge and furrow, can still be made out in the fields between the house and the church at Baddesley. Each peasant was allocated his own strips in the common fields but work – ploughing, harrowing, sowing, reaping and gleaning – was a communal activity.

Above The life of a peasant in the Middle Ages was closely aligned to the seasons, and the church calendar, and some of the most vivid evocations of this life are given in the illuminations of the early 14th-century Luttrell Psalter: ploughing with oxen, sowing, reaping and binding sheaves

Opposite While much larger than Baddesley Clinton's great hall would have been, this at Great Chalfield Manor (also National Trust) shows the archetypal pattern of the English manor house

Managing the manor

Some of the best records of life on the manor of Baddesley belong to the period of John Brome, a well-connected lawyer, who bought the property in 1438, and while owning other lands, seems to have concentrated his activities on Baddesley.

The accounts kept by his faithful bailiff, Mr Boys, between 1442 and 1445 provide a vivid picture of a smaller gentry manorial property that relied less on rents (as the large landowners did) than the lord's ability to manage his property well.

At Baddesley, Brome began by clearing the old selions of thorns and bushes, and invested in hedges and ditches to set himself up as a cattle farmer. Most of the lord's land was devoted to providing produce for Brome's household – wheat for bread, dairy produce, meat, and fruit and vegetables.

The manor's manpower

Mr Boys' accounts and court rolls give evidence of a well-managed and busy estate, with a demesne of some 300 acres. There are mentions of other local families, such as the Shakespeares of Rowington, yeomen or tenant farmers who rented some of the Baddesley lands. There are also men such as John Man and John Sturte, who got into trouble with the manor court over grazing rights, and William Collet, a carpenter who worked on the manor buildings in 1442–58 and sold Brome two oxen in 1444–45.

By the 15th century, the manor had become a more entrepreneurial farming unit that relied on hiring in specialist labourers. The permanent employees seem to be two bailiffs, a waggoner and one other. Temporary specialist labourers, such as smiths, wheelwrights carpenters, thatchers and tilers, were brought in and paid for their services as required. Twelve workers seem to have had specialist labourer status, such as Benedict Cairns, who dug out the fishponds and worked on hedging and harvesting. Another pond-digger was the appropriately named Richard Dyker. Simon Medowe (also well named) had his own plough and waggon, and earned 10s 2d in 1444–45 for ploughing, carting and digging in the quarry. There are glimpses in these papers of sons following fathers; for instance John Boys, paid for ploughwork, was the son of Baddesley's bailiff and later became bailiff himself. Most of those paid for work at this time came from nearby villages and it seems there was only a small population in the village of Baddesley itself.

Village people

The population of a medieval village was complex as the difference between holdings among the serfs could be considerable. Those who had accumulated larger holdings acted as overseers, while at the other end there were men whose holdings were small (known as villeins) and who would labour for others, and the landless cottars, who only laboured for others. While the status of the Tudor agricultural worker had changed from serf to one of free status, they remained tenants of the landowner, working for low wages and paying rent for their cottages, raising their families on small incomes supplemented by their own produce and livestock. The transition to pasture in the 16th century often saw the reduction of village populations as fewer working hands were needed. Indeed the abandoned villages marked on Ordnance Survey maps are as likely to have been due to this conversion to sheep farming as the devastation of the Black Death in the 14th century.

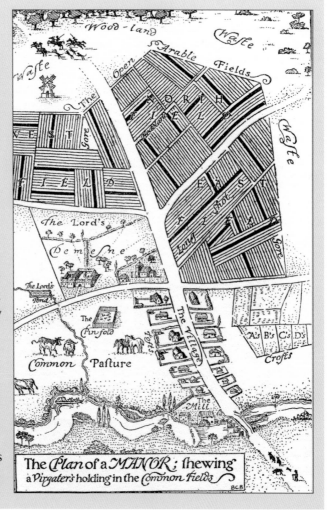

The Plan of a MANOR; shewing a Virgater's holding in the Common Fields

The extended family

Life in the manor house for the landowner, or lord of the manor, depended on the service of others: people to clean, cook, tend the fires, look after the horses and maintain the fabric of the building, as well as administrators to keep accounts and manage the income of the related estates.

The servant body also provided physical security, almost like a small private army, and in turn received the protection of the household. We think of such a community perhaps as 'a household', but until the 19th century the word used in wills and rules setting out the duties of the day, was 'family'. This can be seen at Baddesley Clinton from references in the diaries of Henry Ferrers (1549–1633) to a manservant and his wife, Baldwin and Besse, which hint at how the Ferrers family depended on their servants not just for the comfort of daily life but also for companionship and security (see pages 36–37).

Below and opposite In the Middle Ages domestic staff were exclusively male

Domus aaron speraunt in domino:
adiutor eorum ꝸ protector eorum est.
Qui timent dominum sperauerunt

Men's work

In most periods, until the early 20th century, upper servants would have enjoyed considerable job security – it was not unusual to spend 30 or 40 years working for one master. In the medieval period, much of the menial work was done by young boys, known as grooms, who assisted with the manual jobs (this was long before the word groom became associated with stables). Those who looked after the formal service of meals, bread, meat and wine, were usually male, and the cooks and scullions (who did the washing up) were also male. Women were rarely included amongst servant bodies of landed households until the late 16th and early 17th century. They were employed in the tending of children, but apart from that they were probably only employed in laundry duties, done away from the house.

The heart of the community

A map of 1699 shows the manor house at Baddesley Clinton still at the centre of an interlinked and interdependent rural community (see page 22). Until the late 19th century, the population of the estate would have included many who worked for the lord of the manor as agricultural labourers or estate servants. Livelihoods were reliant on the lord of the manor. The idea of the manorial community, with the squire something of a father figure, was looked at with some nostalgia in the 19th century, with little understanding of what life was actually like for the peasant worker.

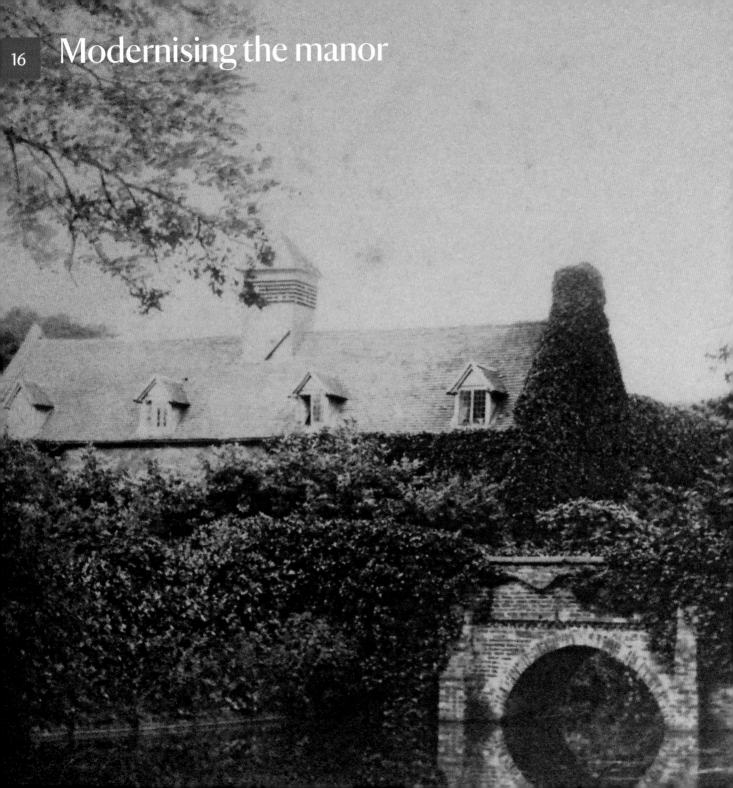

Modernising the manor

While Baddesley Clinton is a picture-postcard manor house, largely of the 15th and 16th centuries, it is easy to overlook the way in which the house was adapted and updated for the life and needs of an 18th-century country gentleman and his family.

By the end of the 17th century the Ferrers family were clearly short of funds, sub-letting the park around the house for many years. In 1712, Edward Ferrers (1678–1729) married Teresa Gibson (d.1734), one of the four daughters of Sir Isaac Gibson of Worcester. She was a wealthy heiress and her money meant that Edward could rebuild the forecourt and farmyard and enclose the south garden; this he did between 1714 and 1722.

'What I have built'

Edward recorded his works in a meticulous note, headed an 'Account of what I have built and altered in and aboute Baddesley house'. He seems to have swept away the 15th-century stone barns and timber gatehouse, which lay much closer to the house, and would have handsomely framed the approach, but appear to have suffered a major fire. He replaced the old timber-framed gatehouse with a new gateway of brick piers topped with urns (replaced in the 19th century). Thus Edward was both updating the outbuildings and improving the farmyard capacity.

The stables, kennels and coach house crowned by a clock tower under a cupola were completed in 1714, and cost £76 17s 7d. The barns were built in 1721–22, and incorporated trusses from older buildings. At the same time he built a 'Woodhouse' and built 'Walls in ye Garden'. His accounts cover many of the small practical details of the self-sufficient country house world of the Georgian gentry, mentioning 'the Hen house and little pigsty adjoining' and 'the house for Emty Bottles'. Payments are recorded for servants' wages, weeding, rat catchers and the purchase of wine and ale, clothing and livestock. These payments illustrate the two layers of working people who sustained the life of a smaller country house: the resident indoor servants and the outdoor servants – teams of gardeners, the coachman, grooms and gamekeepers – who lived on the estate.

Opposite The stables, kennels and coach house were 18th-century additions made by Edward Ferrers after his marriage to a wealthy heiress

Right The Gatehouse Range shown in a print of c.1790–1800 by Henry Jeayes

Serving the manor

Naturally we know much more about how the estate was run in the later 19th century and by whom, thanks to the arrival of the National Census. At around the same time photography became more commonplace and some precious images remain of the staff at Baddesley Clinton.

The servants recorded at Baddesley Clinton Hall in the 1871 census included a married butler James Marriett, who was born in Corfe Castle in Dorset. He would probably have trained elsewhere as a page, footman or under-butler, before becoming a butler (butlers usually came from outside the area while junior servants were recruited locally). The butler's duties included receiving guests, serving the meals and managing the wine cellar, as well as overseeing the cleaning of the fine silver and glass. He may also have acted as a valet for his employer in a relatively small household such as this.

Housekeepers and maids

In the 1881 census the housekeeper is listed as Frances Morris, 74 years old and in charge of the female staff. She also oversaw the cleaning and laundry and buying of provisions. In neither the 1871 nor 1881 census is there mention of a lady's maid, so the senior housemaid may have assisted. Lady Chatterton was said by her husband to be rather frugal about her clothes: 'she always appeared in Society well and becoming

dressed; but many of the dresses that looked the best had cost the least, or were old ones that had been shaped into different fashions modified after her own'. The second Mrs Dering evidently retained a lady's maid in 1918, a servant who acted as companion, dresser and mender of clothes.

The servant faithful

When Edward Dering died, his funeral oration contained references to his regard for his tenants and servants: 'His tenants were treated with a consideration that only members of a family have a right to expect…. His kind and courteous treatment of his servants could not fail to attract the attention of his visitors.' Even allowing for the hyperbole expected at a squire's funeral, this is unusual. Edward left bequests to the local Roman Catholic priest and the parishioners of Baddesley. He also left money and their cottages to his coachman William Herbert and to butler and housekeeper William and Elizabeth Blake. He also left bequests to all his servants including his woodman. Rebecca left £10 to any servants in her employ at the time of her death and also honoured the promises made by Edward about the tied cottages.

William Herbert the coachman photographed after 30 years of service; he appears in the 1901 census aged 70

Opposite top A page of the 1871 census tallying family and servants at Baddesley Clinton

Opposite bottom Baddesley Clinton's domestic staff, c.1905

The undermentioned Houses are situate within the Boundaries of the

[Page 1

No. of Schedule	ROAD, STREET, &c., and No. or NAME of HOUSE	HOUSES In-habit-ed (H.)	HOUSES Unin-habited (U.), or Building (B.)	NAME and Surname of each Person	RELATION to Head of Family	CON-DITION	AGE of Males	AGE of Females	Rank, Profession, or OCCUPATION	WHERE BORN	Whether 1. Deaf-and-Dumb 2. Blind 3. Imbecile or Idiot 4. Lunatic
1	Netherwood Heath	1		Harriet Brown	Head	M		46 46	Farmer of 190 acres employing 5 men	Worcestersh. Yardley	
				Henry do	Son	Unm	22		Farmers Son	do Kings Norton	
				Thomas do	Son	Unm	20		do do	do do	
				William do	Son	Unm	19		do do	Warwickshire Baddesley	
				Jacob do	Son	Unm	16		do do	do do	
				Samuel do	Son	Unm	8		Scholar	do do	
				Joseph do	Son	Unm	4			do do	
				Emily A. Clarke	Serv	Unm		16	General Serv. Domestic	Worcestersh. Elcot	
2	Baddesley Hall Stable Yard	1		Mathew Cox	Head	Mar	63		Coachman	Beds Salford	
				Henrietta do	Wife	Mar		63	Coachman's wife	do Cryinefield	
				Jeremiah do	Son	Unm	30		Clerk &c	do Salford	
3	Baddesley Hall	1		Marmion E. Ferrers	Head	Mar	57		Magistrate Landowner	Somerset Bristol	
				Rebecca D. do	Wife	Mar		41		Ireland	
4	.			Edward H. Dering	Head	Mar	47		Late of the Coldstream James	Kent Pluckley	
				Georgiana Lady Chatterton	Wife	Mar		61		Arlingland	
				James Marriott	Serv	Mar	51		Butler Domestic Serv	Dorset Corfe Castle	
				George Tho Spittaway	Serv	Unm	32		Footman Domestic Serv	Warwicksh. Halloall Temple	
				Flora Thomas	Serv	Unm		21	Housemaid do do	Herts Boughton Monchelsea	
				Esther Carter	Serv	Unm		17	do do do	Warwicksh. Burford	
5	Haywood Lodge	1		Swain Wilson	Head	Mar	82		Woodman	do Solihull	
				Mary do	Wife	Mar		77	Woodman's Wife	do Broughill	
				Caroline do	Niece Visitor	Unm		21	Unemployed	do Solihull	
	Total of Houses..	4				Total of Males and Females..	13	9			Eng– Sheet A.

* Draw the pen through such of the words as are inappropriate.

Servants in residence

In 1881, under the housekeeper were the cook, Annie Harrison, and two housemaids, Esther Carter, 27, and Elizabeth Hammond, 19, both unmarried, as junior domestic servants tended to be. There was also a coachman, William Herbert, then 50, who appears in photographs as a distinguished-looking man. He worked for the family for many years and was married with a family. A 17-year-old groom Frederic Herbert, presumably William's son, would have probably lived over the stables, partly for security, as he is listed as resident not at his father's house but in the hall. There was a head gardener, Henry Morris, aged 75, who probably employed other young men who didn't live in the complex around the hall.

Growing for pleasure

The setting of Baddesley Clinton has always been important to the enjoyment of the life of its owners and visitors. As observed by the Elizabethan squire of Baddesley, Henry Ferrers (1549–1633), the function of the garden and orchards around the moated manor was to provide the family with pleasure as well as food for the table.

Some of the garden's elements were originally more functional. In the medieval era fish were stocked in the stewponds to provide food for the household. There are accounts for the excavation and stocking of the pool in 1444, and more stock referred to in 1456–57. The Great Pool, which forms part of an attractive walk today, is thought to have been a millpond, and also to have been part of the fish stocking process.

These features have all been brought into the pleasure grounds over time, especially from the mid-18th century onwards. In 1748 Thomas Ferrers 'made the Lo[w]er garden and the new Leyd [laid] out Turf Walks', the walks presumably around the Great Pool. In 1752, he had built a 'Colde Bath' reached by an ornamental path, and he was also a busy tree-planter – in the same year he added new gates and a palisade fence to the entrance court. Later members of the Ferrers family also made their mark in the park, and just beyond the Lakeside Walk is the wildflower meadow, with its cowslips and primroses, which was created in the 1950s by Thomas Weaving Ferrers-Walker on the site of an 18th-century orchard.

A more formal approach

The Walled Garden was created in the early 18th century as an enclosed formal garden on the sunnier side of the house. Little survives of any early planting, as much of the garden was simplified from the 1920s onwards. But it appears that it reached a highpoint in the early 20th century, as watercolours of 1915 survive in the house that show a wonderful traditional English flower garden in the Gertrude Jekyll spirit. It was divided from the moat by a tall yew hedge, which at the time was tended by a team of gardeners, under head gardener John Chinn, whom Rebecca had to lay off in 1923 as her income declined. In the 1980s the National

Opposite Trees reflected in the Stew Pond once stocked with fish for the table

Trust re-introduced the sundial and created formal rose beds around it, and also planted some traditional apple trees.

The courtyard garden features beds modelled on the mascles (lozenges with a lozenge-shaped hole at the centre) in the Ferrers coat of arms and planted in red and gold. The yew mostly survive from the 19th-century planting.

Walks in the woods

The woodland to the west was planted out as pleasure grounds in the 19th century, with walks created around the ancient stew ponds. A tithe plan from 1870 shows a short, yew-lined carriage drive running around the stew ponds and Long Ditch. Created for Rebecca, she continued to use the drive well into the 20th century.

In many ways the development of the lakeside walk is similar to that of the gardens, from utilitarian beginnings to modest pleasure grounds, absorbing but not obliterating the past.

The meadow has been one of the most important contributions to the garden's recent history, demonstrating a sympathetic feeling for the past and adding to Baddesley Clinton's undeniably romantic atmosphere.

Above The Walled Garden in 1915; by A. E. Lilley

Below Brightly coloured dahlias in the Walled Garden

Opposite The estate map of Baddesley Clinton made in 1699 by William Adam

Left Sheep have grazed the fields around Baddesley Clinton since the 16th century

One of the things that gives Baddesley Clinton its particular character in the 21st century is its long history as the focus of an agricultural community.

All the farmland here was originally carved out of the ancient Forest of Arden. Agricultural activity has ebbed and flowed over the centuries and shaped the landscape. A small village, possibly never very large, disappeared as grazing replaced open-field farming and different patterns of agriculture evolved in the 18th and 19th centuries.

Henry Ferrers appears to have been responsible for the creation of a deer park – an important signifier of status and source of venison, a meat for the privileged. A map by Christopher Saxton made in 1579 shows Baddesley Clinton as a simple settlement but by the 1637 revision, Baddesley is shown with a substantial fenced park.

Mapping the manor

A 1676 lease of 'Baddesley Clynton' mentions 'the manor house of Baddesley … together with all lands and rights pertaining to the same, and lands called the Orchard, Oake yard, the garden, Barne field, Church field, Moat field, Lint alias Line field, Lodg field, Foure fields, Mill field adjoining to the Walleis, Great Walleis, Milking yard, Mill meadow, Dear meadow, Park meadow, Black meadow, Millholme, Mill pools, the Moate.'

The 1699 estate map drawn up by William Adam (opposite) records the manor and its outbuildings at the centre of a dense network of field boundaries. The field names closest to the manor house still include Church Field, Barne Field, Mill Field, Milking Yard and Mill Meadow, while four large fields to the north are marked as 'pieces of the parke'; the surviving ancient forest of Hay Wood still dominates the estate's eastern part.

A parkland setting

The property came into the hands of the National Trust in 1980. The aim of today's landscape management is to develop an appropriate setting for the house while also encouraging wildlife and increasing visitors' pleasure in this intimate and historic Warwickshire landscape.

There is an 1840s tithe plan for the parish of Baddesley Clinton which provides the first detailed survey since 1699. Several fields north of the house, adjacent to the drive, continued to be known as parks, namely First Park, Home Park, Long Park and Great Park, but they were all in arable use, except for First Park, which was meadow.

During the 18th century, the Ferrers family continued actively planting trees to improve the parkland around the manor house. An early 1700s list of tree planting, 'Mr Ferriss's Timber at Badgley', refers to ash, chestnut, elm and poplar, and in 1744 Thomas Ferrers recorded: 'I planted two Clumps of Beech trees upon Kingswood Common near The Sand pitts … planting 120 in each clump'.

Right Church Walk on the Baddesley Clinton estate

Wartime cutbacks

A 1923 survey of the estate carried out on Rebecca's death, by land agent and surveyor E. H. Tipping reviewed the possibility of selling the house and estate, but 'we possibly could let on a repairing lease to a rich American'. He noted sadly that 'the large area of woodland, the major portion of which is known as Hay Wood extending to 258 acres ... is practically denuded of timber, the Government during the War having taken over all the timber then fit to cut'.

A slice of old England for sale

In 1939 The Baddesley Clinton estate was put up for sale. The sales particulars described the estate as comprising 1,350 acres, incorporating 320 acres of woodland and plantations, while the gardens and grounds included walks, lawns, shrubberies, ornamental trees, a productive walled kitchen garden and two heated glasshouses. The estate was also described as having a two-acre lake, parkland, spinnies (small clumps of trees) and pasture land. The tenant farm units within the landholding were listed: Netherwood Heath Farm; Dun Calf Farm; Convent Farm; Hay Wood Farm; Green Farm; Lyons Farm; Wood Corner Farm.

Present plans

The landscape that frames the idyllic ancient manor house is increasingly recognised for its environmental importance. Currently, after much research and advice from experts, there is a project supported by Natural England to restore the traditional character of the fields and park. Some areas of trees have been thinned and others planted to reinstate important historic views that had been lost. Traditional cleft-oak park-palings have been erected in some places and hedgerows restored in others, while ponds have been cleared.

People, Plots and Puzzles

A variety of architectural features and building materials reflect the changing fashions and uses of the manor house

Many people have passed through Baddesley Clinton, some publicly others surreptitiously, so it's hardly surprising to learn that it has been the scene of shadowy deeds. Just as intriguing is the building itself, but there are clues to its past if you know where to look.

There has been a manor house here since before the Norman Conquest (see page 2). Records survive which tell us how the property changed hands. But it's in the 15th century that things start to get interesting.

The murder of a squire

In 1438, we know that the manor was bought by a Warwick lawyer, John Brome. In November 1468, Brome was murdered in the porch of the church of the Carmelite monastery known as the Whitefriars in London, after a quarrel over property with John Herthill. Herthill was the steward of Richard Neville, Earl of Warwick, known to history as the Kingmaker.

John Brome's tomb inscription described the terrible event: 'Lo! Here lies as dust the body of John Brome, a noble and learned man, skilled in the law of the Realm, a child of genius, witness the County of Warwick, who fell by the sword in this church, slain at the time of the mass by the hands of wicked men.' A strange twist in the tale is a codicil in John's will: 'I do forgive my son Thomas, who, when he sawe me runne through in ye Whitefriers church porch, laughed and smiled att itt.' What prompted Thomas's odd behaviour is entirely lost to history, and it fell to a second son, Nicholas, who inherited Baddesley Clinton after the death of his mother, to avenge his father's death.

In 1471, Nicholas (d.1517) met Herthill on his way to Barford near Warwick, and in Longbridge Field 'sett upon him, and in a duel slew him'. Nicholas certainly seems to have had a fiery temper, as, before 1485, according to his descendant, the Elizabethan lawyer and scholar, Henry Ferrers the Antiquary (see pages 30–31), he 'slew ye minister of Baddesley Church finding him in his plor [parlour] chockinge his wife under ye chinne [flirting with her], and to expiatt these bloody offences and crimes he built ye steeple [at Baddesley Clinton church] and raysed ye church body ten foote higher.... I have seene ye Kinge's pardon for itt, and ye Pope's p[ar]don and his penaunce injoined him.... He also builded Packwood Church.'

Enter the Ferrers family

Any visitor to Baddesley Clinton will have a sense of its many occupants and guests. The story of the estate didn't start with a Ferrers, but it is the generations of this family that have left their mark, building, remodelling, renovating and restoring, leaving the patchwork you see today.

The Baddesley Clinton estate passed through the marriage of Nicholas Brome's daughter Constance to Edward (later Sir Edward) Ferrers (c.1468–1535). The property then passed through 13 generations of the Ferrers family until the middle of the 20th century.

The first Ferrers

Edward was knighted at Tournai, having led a band of 100 men as part of a campaign that resulted in its capture in 1513 by Henry VIII, making it the only Belgian city ever to have been ruled by England. In 1520 he was a commissioner overseeing footmen at the Field of Cloth of Gold, the scene of negotiations between King Henry VIII and King Francis I of France to increase the bond of friendship following an Anglo-French treaty of 1514. He also served his king at the meeting with the Holy Roman Emperor, Charles V, at Gravelines.

Edward was High Sheriff of Warwickshire in 1513 and 1518, and High Sheriff of Worcestershire in 1528 until his death in 1535 (unusual as it was normally a 12-month post). He served in the Reformation Parliament of 1529 as a knight. He died on 29 August 1535 and was buried at

Baddesley Clinton, where his wife later installed a window to his and her memory. In his will, he listed lands in Cambridgeshire, Hertfordshire, Kent, Rutland, Staffordshire and Warwickshire, as well as some tenements beside London Wall. His eldest son had died in 1526 and the heir was his grandson Edward (1526–64), who married Bridget (d.1582), a daughter of Lord Windsor. Their son

Above The Ferrers family was responsible for the creation of Baddesley Clinton as you see it today, with major remodellings in the 17th and 18th centuries

Henry (1549–1633) was an active lawyer, whose impressive historical researches earned him the nickname the Antiquary (see pages 30–31). He and his son Edward (1585–1651) carried out a number of remodellings at Baddesley Clinton, introducing oak panelling, carved overmantels and stained glass, giving the house much of the character we see today.

This seate and soyle from Saxon Bade,
    a man of honest fame,
Who held it in the Saxon's tyme of
    Badesley took the name.
When Edward King the Confessor
    did weare the English crowne
The same was then possest by Wrox,
    a man of some renowne,
And England being conquered in lot it did alight
To Geoffrey Wirce of noble birth
    an Andegavian knighte.
A member hamlet of this whyle of
    Hampton nere at hand
With Hampton so to Mouldray went,
    as all the Wirce's land.
Noew Moulbray lord of all doth part these two,
    and gives this one
To Bisege; in that name it runs awhile
    and then is gone
To Clinton as his heyre who leaves it to a younger son;
And in that time Baddesley Clinton was begun.
From them agayne, by wedding of their
    heyre at first it came
To Conisby, and after him to Foukes,
    who weds the same.
From Foukes to Dudley by a sale,
    and so to Burdet past,
To Metley next by Metley's will it came
    to Brome at last.
Brome honours much the place,
    and after some descents of Bromes
To Ferrers, for a daughter's parte of theirs
    in match it comes.
In this last name it lasteth still, and so long longer shall
As God shall please who is the Lord,
    and King, and God of all.

An account in verse by Henry the Antiquary of how
Baddesley Clinton came to the Ferrers family

Henry the Antiquary

One of the most beguiling and human figures in the history of Baddesley Clinton is Henry Ferrers, an eager historian who was later nicknamed the Antiquary. He was considered a great expert on the history not just of his own family, but also of his county.

It was Henry who introduced much of the 16th-century heraldic glass in celebration of his ancestry. He was especially praised by the famous county historian, Sir William Dugdale, author of *Antiquities of Warwickshire* (1656), who observed of him: 'for his eminent knowledge of Antiquities, gave fair luster to that ancient and noble Family, whereof he was no small ornament, is yet of high esteem in these parts'.

Henry was the son of Edward Ferrers and Bridget, the daughter of Lord Windsor. Two brothers, Ferdinando and Edward, died fighting in the Low Countries. The Ferrers family were struggling financially and in 1563 Edward had entered into an agreement with his brother-in-law, who took over the management of his estates. The family seemed to have settled at Hewell Grange for a time. Henry's father died the next year when he was still a minor, so the estates were administered first by his mother's brother, Lord Windsor, and later his mother's second husband, Andrew Ognall. Educated at Hart Hall in Oxford (which later became Hertford College), Henry trained to be a lawyer and was admitted to Middle Temple in 1572.

In 1574, Henry came into his estates and, following sales of his other properties, he was able to begin a programme of improvement of the main house, including alterations to the Gatehouse Range such as new windows and a new roof. These works seem to have included the rebuilding of the East Range containing the new Great Hall, and new staircases and first-floor corridors to allow for more privacy on that floor.

Left Henry the Antiquary was responsible for the windows and roof of the Gatehouse Range

'Henrie Ferrars of Baddesley, a man both for parentage and for knowledge of antiquity very commendable: and my especiall friend: who both in this place and also else where hath at all times courteously shewed me the right way when I was out, and from his candle, as it were, hath lighted mine.'

William Camden, historian

Keeping the faith

As we have seen, a country manor was at the centre of its own little world and at Baddesley from the Reformation onwards this was a Roman Catholic world. The solid walls, the moat, the distance from town, made Baddesley Clinton a natural hiding place for Catholics in the 16th century.

In the late 1580s Henry seems to have been struggling financially, and was even briefly imprisoned for attacking a man in Lincoln's Inn, which may have been over money. We know he made the decision to lease out

Baddesley Clinton from time to time. In 1590 he rented the house to the daughters of Lord Vaux, who were ardent Catholics. After the Act of Uniformity of 1587, it was a treasonable offence to be or to harbour in your house a Roman Catholic priest. The Vaux sisters allowed a number of English Jesuit priests to use Baddesley Clinton as a base for missionary work and created hiding places for them and their belongings, to which they could retreat if the house was visited by the priest hunters.

They did this apparently without Henry's knowledge. He was either a total innocent, a

Above The Gunpowder Plotters; Guy Fawkes hid the gunpowder in Henry's house in London

very lucky man or a person with friends in high places, for he also sold a lease on his London house to Thomas Percy, one of the conspirators of the Gunpowder Plot. It was in that very house that Guy Fawkes stored the gunpowder used in the attempt to blow up the Houses of Parliament.

Hiding places

Baddesely Clinton's priest hole lay below the floor level of the house and can still be seen today in the floor of the kitchen. Its creation is attributed to one Nicholas Owen, a small man, known as Little John, who trained as a carpenter and was a personal servant of Father John Gerard, the Jesuit Superior. Father Gerard described it as 'a very cleverly built sort of cave'. Back then, the only way to access this was via the shaft of the garderobe, or privy.

Loyal protectors

Baddesley Clinton's tenants would have brought their own staff with them, and in the case of the Vaux sisters it served them well to do so. Their servants were risking their lives alongside their employers when they looked after priests or attended mass, but they remained loyal. Father Gerard related: 'There were four of them [priest hunters] altogether, with swords drawn, and they were battering the door to force an entrance. But a faithful servant held them back, otherwise we should all have been caught … the servants held the door fast. They said the mistress of the house, a widow, was not yet up, but was coming down to answer them.'

Hidden history

Father John Gerard left a memoir of a raid on a private house by the priest hunters in October 1591, which is now thought to be an account of a raid on Baddesley Clinton, during which he and Father Garnet and seven other priests hid for four hours in this very place.

'It was about five o'clock the following morning. I was making my meditation, Father Southwell was beginning Mass and the rest were at prayer, when suddenly I heard a great uproar outside the main door. Then I heard a voice shouting and swearing at a servant who was refusing them entrance.... But a faithful servant held them back, otherwise we should all have been caught. Father Southwell heard the din. He guessed what it was all about, and slipped off his vestments and stripped the altar bare. While he was doing this, we laid hold of all our personal belongings: nothing was left to betray the presence of a priest. Even our boots and swords were hidden away – they would have roused suspicions if none of the people they belonged to were to be found. Our beds presented a problem: as they were still warm and merely covered in the usual way preparatory to being made, some of us went and turned the beds and put them cold side up to delude anyone who put his hand in to feel them....

Right **A Catholic priest on the rack**

Opposite **The priest hole was accessed by the garderobe, or privy**

Vt. quibus excepti domibus mysteria Christi
Egerunt, quosque à funestro schismate sanctæ
Iunxere Ecclesiæ, prodant, et talia multa
Distendunt miseros diris cruciatibus artus

'Outside the ruffians were bawling and yelling, but the servants held the door fast. They said the mistress of the house, a widow, was not yet up, but coming down at once to answer them. This gave us enough time to stow ourselves in a very cleverly built sort of cave. At last the leopards were let in. They tore madly through the whole house, searched everywhere, pried with candles into the darkest corners. They took four hours over the work but fortunately chanced on nothing....

'When they had gone, and gone a good way, so that there was no danger of their turning back suddenly as they sometimes do, a lady came and called us out of our den, not one but several Daniels. The hiding place was below ground level: the floor was covered with water and I was standing with my feet in it all the time. Father Garnet was there, also Father Southwell and Father Oldcorne, ... Father Stanney, and myself, two secular priests and two or three laymen.'

Three of the named Jesuits were later executed for treason, a barbaric execution to modern ears that included being hung by the neck till nearly dead, drawn, or disembowelled while still alive, and then cut into four quarters. Father Garnet was captured in 1606 and executed after the Gunpowder Plot, which he had known about through the confession of Robert Catesby. He had opposed and advised against it, but under the sacrament of confession he was unable to expose it. His Baddesley protector Anne Vaux herself rushed from the crowd to try to speak to him on the day of his execution in London. In his last minutes an onlooker shouted out accusing him of being married to Anne Vaux. Such was the sympathy that the crowds, both Catholic and Protestant, felt for Garnet, that they refused to let him be cut down to be drawn while still alive.

Henry's accounts

'For pleasure 1. a garden 2. an orchard 3. a galorie 4. bookes.'

Henry the Antiquary

Below Henry the Antiquary noted in his diary how pleased he was with the fireplace in his bedchamber

Opposite Henry the Antiquary listed his books as one of life's great pleasures

Papers left behind by Henry the Antiquary reveal much about the ordinary habits of the life and family at Baddesley Clinton; they reveal preoccupations with meals and interior decoration, and also the relationship between the father and son and their servants.

Henry left a range of notebooks and lists, dating from 1600 onwards, which reveal his sheer enjoyment of Baddesley Clinton. He makes notes on what he possesses: 'For profit.... For storage.... For pleasure.... For necessity.' Henry's son Edward married Anne Peyto in 1611, and Henry retained for himself half the manor house, fishing rights in the moat and the right to remove wood for fuel, while giving over the rest of the house to his son and daughter-in-law.

A grandson, also Henry, was born in 1616. Edward undertook some further major works, beginning well within his father's lifetime, creating the new Great Parlour on the first floor and adding useful corridors. Scraps of Henry the elder's diaries from the 1620s survive, recording his delight in the new works, including the carved chimneypiece for his great chamber, or bedroom. His accounts suggest that he occupied some of the first-floor rooms: he describes his bedchamber having curtains and canopies 'of orange colour'. He also describes the varying uses of a bedchamber, which had enough suitable furniture to be used for dining: 'my son dined with me in my bedchamber. We had butter, a capon [rooster] and boiled eggs and apples'.

Henry's diaries record the small details of everyday life at Baddesley Clinton, including having his bed warmed by a servant girl 'Besse' before his use, and he muses on the pleasures of taking a little tobacco. All in all Henry comes across as an intelligent and agreeable fellow, who delighted in all the human pleasures afforded by his family home and would have welcomed guests warmly if not extravagantly.

Civil War travails

Edward and Anne had four children of whom only one survived, Henry. The fourth was stillborn and was buried in the same coffin as her mother, who died in childbirth in 1618. Edward's marriage settlement secured much of Anne's money, which may be the reason he didn't marry again. Edward lived in rooms on the ground floor with his servant Baldwin and Baldwin's wife Besse, the aforementioned bed-warmer.

Henry the Antiquary died in 1633, and a year after inheriting Baddesley Clinton Edward rebuilt the chancel of the Anglican parish church, and made some alterations to the house. He was High Sheriff from 1639 to 1641. He tried to avoid taking sides during the Civil War, as Warwickshire was under Parliamentary control. In 1634, Parliamentary troops came and took a 'gelding of a bright bay colour' and '1 gray coloured mare'. They ransacked the house and took away a 'plush saddle', gunpowder and a musket, a Geneva bible and 'many linens out of ye drying chamber'. Later they came back and took two oxen and eight milk cows. Many houses were stripped bare, but Edward's brother-in-law Sir Edward Peyto was deputy to Lord Brooke, the leading Parliamentarian in Warwickshire, which may have given them some protection. It is possible, despite the reputation of the family's unbroken Catholic line, that Edward conformed to avoid greater losses.

A puzzling building

The sight of a moated manor house makes an immediate and compelling impression on visitors today. The house is in many ways a beautiful patchwork, built in different phases in the 15th and 16th centuries, with alterations in the 17th, 18th and 19th centuries.

The Ferrers, although certainly an old family and proud 'gentry', were never rich, and the changes made are typical modernisations and improvements one might expect in a house of this size. Had they been richer, a bigger house might have been built elsewhere and the manor house abandoned, divided into cottages for tenant farmers, or perhaps even part demolished to form an eye-catcher in the park, as at Scotney Castle in Kent.

We are grateful that they didn't, so that today we may walk through and around this delightful house, glimpsing the efforts of owners and tenants through the centuries to make it more secure, more comfortable, or perhaps easier to run. The puzzles of an old building are inherent and it could be said that they exist today partly for our amusement and pleasure as we try to puzzle out the story, putting together the pieces of evidence is as engaging as the best jigsaw.

Left A mixture of medieval in the Gatehouse Range, mid-17th-century in the middle section and Tudor-style block work from the Victorian period

Below The Gatehouse in the Entrance Range on the north side of the manor house

Ancient history

It is thought that there has been a manor house on this site from around 1230, shortly after the manor came into the hands of the de Clinton family (see page 2). This would have comprised a group of buildings surrounded by the moat and entered originally on the eastern side. Indeed, there is evidence of a second moat, which would have provided greater security and increased the sense of grandeur.

The medieval gatehouse would have served as the entrance to the original great hall and would have been a capacious timber-framed structure and would have been located largely in what is now the courtyard garden of the house, standing on the western side of the island. This had a two-storey cross wing which would have included the great chamber of the lord of the manor with a secure room underneath for storage (in many houses there might be a chapel attached to the great chamber as well as additional bedchambers). The kitchen at this date was probably a free-standing structure to the north of the original hall.

There is little left of this early house. The earliest visible elements date to the 15th and 16th centuries, and these have been partly absorbed into later phases. It seems that the original medieval hall and other buildings (which seem to have survived as what is called the Old Kitchen in a 1760 inventory) may have been demolished at the end of the 18th century. Nonetheless it should be remembered that the 13th-century moat dictated both the footprint and architectural proportion of the house we see today and any earlier buildings.

The manor in the 15th century

When the manor was acquired by John Brome in 1459, there was clearly a programme of rebuilding. This included the building of a new L-shaped chamber block, alongside the cross wing, which provided additional chambers and appears to have had three rooms on each level and a garderobe on the ground floor. The first floor was jettied out on the moat side; the south arm of this new chamber block had just one room on the first floor, which was possibly the new great chamber (now the Chapel). One of the towers from this period of building is located on the south-east corner and encloses a staircase. The ceiling structure of the Sacristy reveals part of the 15th-century work. These rooms would have functioned with the existing great hall and cross wing.

Right The south side of the house: the Chapel and Sacristy are located above the 18th-century toilet block projection; right of this is an original 15th-century staircase tower

of the courtyard. A new staircase leading off from the Great Hall was added and the circulation around the building was made easier, with the emphasis on convenience, comfort and warmth.

17th-century installations

In the mid-17th century panelling was put up in the south-east rooms of the house, and a new Great Parlour (a grand dining and reception room) was created by a rearrangement of the dividing walls over the north-facing Gatehouse; this included the creation of a new mullioned and transomed window over the Gatehouse (a mullion is the upright window division and the transom the one that goes across) and the barrel-vaulted ceiling in the Great Parlour.

The 16th-century manor house

The cross wing was rebuilt in the period 1526–36 by Edward Ferrers, who constructed a masonry range and upgraded the earlier chamber block by continuing the stone facing along the entire south front. He also built a new sewer (at moat level) along the whole of the south face of the house. A new gatehouse range was added, providing a secure entrance to the north, with a projecting drawbridge bay, a porter's lodge and other rooms.

By the later 16th century, tastes had changed again and in the 1570s and 1580s Henry Ferrers constructed a new east range, including the present Great Hall, completing the fourth side

Above The connecting east range built by Henry Ferrers containing the Great Hall with its substantial chimney; he also added the staircase off the Great Hall lit by the large window in the middle of the range

Right The mullions and transoms of the Great Parlour window overlooking the courtyard

The porch was still gabled after this work, the attractive battlements not added until the 19th century. A finely carved armorial overmantel commemorating the family's lineage and marital alliances was installed in the Great Parlour. This was moved in the 18th century to its present position in the Great Hall. The east wall's timber frame and jetty were replaced with brickwork, from the south corner staircase tower to the chimney of the Great Hall. The originally open galleries on the first floor associated with the 15th-century chamber block (on your left as you enter the courtyard) were enclosed with brickwork and given windows.

18th-century evolutions

In the 18th century, there was no major architectural revolution in the house, rather a consolidation of the supporting buildings to satisfy a sporting gentleman's interests, and to improve the agricultural profitability of the property. In 1703 the south range was re-roofed and the timber-framed walls built up in brick. The estate buildings through which the house is approached by most visitors were largely built in the early 18th century by Edward Ferrers. The 'nether stable' was built or altered in 1713, and the Coach House in 1714 (at a cost of £76 17s 7d), as well as the clock tower which crowned it. The barn, where the restaurant is located today, was built in 1721–22, along with a woodhouse and garden walls. A new brick bridge to the house was built in the 1720s.

Thomas Ferrers carried out some works in 1747–48, including converting the room then used as the servants' hall, presumably since the 17th century, into the kitchen and building a new hearth and chimney (this is the kitchen you see today). This chimney rose through what is now known as the Sacristy, and was removed in 1940. In 1749, he 'Painted the Little Parlour and Put a new Window in itt' and in the following year, he 'made up and floord the Great Parlor'.

In around 1752, Thomas Ferrers, 'put up the Chimny piece in the Hall from the Great dining room' (which is assumed to be the Great Parlour) and added a plaster ceiling (this was removed after a serious fire in 1940 to reveal the 16th-century beams). Thomas is thought to have perhaps been responsible for pulling down the old timber-framed great hall. In the 1790s, Edward Ferrers carried out some further modest improvements, including re-facing the eastern part of the entrance front in stone and rebuilding the north-east corner of the house (the present Drawing Room). Some of the brick facing inside the courtyard probably also dates from this period.

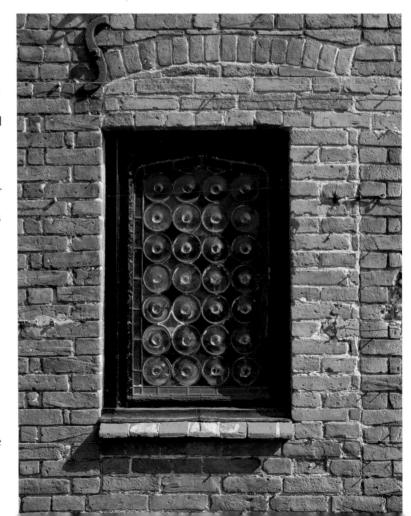

Below Window and brickwork of the 18th-century stables, showing the original size of the window

Improve or preserve?

Left The view through the Gatehouse to the service wing, Tudor in style but not added until the end of the 19th century

Opposite Thomas and Undine; the couple devoted a great deal of time and energy to restoring Baddesley Clinton

In the 19th century, additional servants' areas were created in order to make the house function more efficiently. In more modern times, the overriding concern has been sensitive restoration and preservation.

In the late 19th century a new addition was made to the south-west range, improving the servants' offices and accommodation. According to Henry Norris, who wrote a detailed history of Baddesley Clinton: 'additional buildings, adjoining this [original] wing and extending into the courtyard were erected in 1890 in black and white timber work by the late Mr Dering, and these whether considered artistically or substantially would do credit to mediaeval days. Yet the design was his own, and the workmen local artisans only.'

But in the 20th century a new fashion holds the image of the house: the romance of the past, and a new, almost scientific approach to preserving what has survived. In 1940, Thomas Ferrers-Walker re-created the Sacristy and removed the 18th-century chimneystack (see page 51). He and his wife Undine personally stripped back the many layers of paint in certain rooms, repaired the timberwork after a fire in the Great Hall in 1940 and removed the plaster ceiling in the same room.

Since the house came into the hands of the National Trust in 1980, the emphasis has been on restoration, conservation and repair, and making the house safe and enjoyable for its many visitors from around the British Isles and indeed the world.

In the Present Manor

Walking around the house, we find each room is like a window onto the centuries. History is expressed in their form and their furnishings, but not everything is always quite as it seems.

The Great Hall

The Great Hall is a room of many uses. It was contrived by Henry the Antiquary, who built most of the east range, as a reception room and for larger entertainments, and he introduced the handsome oak panelling and armorial stained glass. Formal dining would have been in the first-floor Great Parlour (see page 54) and family dining would have taken place in a more private space, so the Great Hall , although re-created after the medieval fashion, was quite different in function to the great halls of medieval manor houses.

A Georgian gentleman

Thomas Ferrers (1713–60), whose portrait hangs in the Great Hall, married Margaret Kempson from a local family of Henley-in-Arden in 1737 but did not move into Baddesley Clinton until 1747. He established a library at the house and also carried out alterations to the interiors. His choices show a degree of interest in the ancient manor house as an admired historic building. He moved the overmantel from the room over the entrance (the Great Parlour) to the Great Hall (in 1752 he wrote: 'put up the Chimny piece in the Hall from the Great dining room' and in 1754 that he 'Floor'd and shelvd the Closet by the little Parlour' and he 'Floor'd and made a new Door to ye Little Parlor').

Thomas created a central door opposite the chimneypiece that opened onto the courtyard garden, so making the Great Hall an impressive entrance hall. Whilst having an eye to the past,

Thomas was also a bit of a moderniser and added a plain plaster ceiling concealing the great 16th-century timbers, not revealed until after the fire of 1940.

When Thomas died, the house appears not to have been richly furnished; an inventory of the Great Hall lists: 'One Long Table; Two Mahogany Oval Tables; One Card Table; one eight day clock and case and bust; Fifteen Pictures one Indian Picture and one Old map; One Lamp.'

Opposite The Great Hall is the centrepiece of Henry the Antiquary's medieval remodellings

Piecing the fireplace

One of the most intriguing puzzles at Baddesely Clinton is the curious framing of the finely carved fireplace surround in the Great Hall. It is derived, as much carved decoration was from the 1570s to the early 1600s, from the printed designs in Sebastiano Serlio's *Five Books of Architecture*. This fireplace was moved to this room from the Great Parlour on the first floor in 1752, and it seems that at that time, the parts of the upright sections to either side of it were re-installed in the wrong order. This is something very unlikely to have occurred in the early 1600s when it was being made, but a Georgian mason would not have had the engraving (pictured right) to hand for the re-assembly.

first father-in-law, Edward Ferrers. She also painted the heraldic shields above the panelling after her marriage to Edward Dering in 1885.

In honour of husbands

Rebecca painted the portraits of her two husbands that hang in this room: *The Squire's Evening Walk* (Marmion, see page 9) and *The Philosopher's Morning Walk* (Edward, also page 9), both in their idiosyncratic, old-fashioned dress.

Photographs from the 1920s show that the room was little changed from the painted view until the sale of contents during the 1930s. Some pieces were bought back by Thomas Ferrers-Walker, but relatively few of the original contents can be seen in this room. The long table, recorded in this room in 1760, can be seen at nearby Packwood House.

The Quartet at repose

A delightful oil painted by Rebecca Ferrers in 1870 shows the Quartet relaxing in the Great Hall. Marmion Ferrers sits to one side of the fire; Lady Chatterton sits on the other, writing a letter; Edward Dering sits reading, but has his head held as if he is listening to one of the others speaking or reading out loud. Rebecca depicted herself in riding costume, arranging flowers. Tables and sofas are draped in velvet, with books piled high. The painting sums up the friends' shared interests: books, old furniture, paintings and china, all in an oak-panelled room with daylight dappled through 16th-century armorial stained glass.

Although much of the furniture in the room today was brought in by the Ferrers-Walkers, it is still easy to see and feel the connection of this room to that picture. The stained glass in the large windows facing the courtyard was installed by Henry the Antiquary; that of the central window by Rebecca Dering in 1894 to commemorate her two husbands and her

The unicorn's horn

By the door to the Entrance Hall is one of the treasures of the house, described by Fletcher Moss during his visit in 1906: 'In the corner is a singular twisted horn of great age and about eight feet long. About the year 1400, the French ambassador presented, amongst other gifts, a unicorn's horn to Lord de Ferrers – an allusion to the family crest – and this has always been traditionally regarded as the same horn. It is really the horn of a narwhal, or sea-unicorn.' A painting by Rebecca depicts Marmion holding said horn.

The Dining and Drawing Rooms

The stained glass in the Dining Room shows the arms of Henry Ferrers (d.1526) and his wife Katherine Hampden, the arms of Sir Edward Ferrers (d.1535) and Constance Brome and Henry Hampden and his wife, Elizabeth, daughter of Sir Edward Ferrers. It is furnished with handsome pieces of 17th- and 18th-century oak furniture acquired by Thomas Ferrers-Walker in the 1940s, which was when the stone surround of the fireplace was installed.

The Drawing Room is part of the house that was rebuilt in around 1790. The glass and oak panelling and armorial chimneypiece were re-used from other rooms in the house. There are two stained-glass windows, one 16th-century, the other introduced in the 1890s by Rebecca in memory of her two husbands.

Adjoining the Great Hall are the Drawing Room and the Dining Room, the latter used as such from the 18th century onwards. The Dining Room was originally part of the porter's lodge of the medieval house and was later fitted out as a family parlour in the 1630s, in effect a private dining room, as guests would be entertained in the Great Parlour.

Above The view through the arched doorway into the Dining Room

Right A detail of the Georgian walnut writing desk in the Drawing Room

Opposite The Quartet in the Great Hall, by Rebecca, 1870

Henry Ferrers' Bedroom

As you climb the main staircase from the Great Hall, added in the 16th century, you come first to the bedroom fitted out for Henry the Antiquary. The elaborate carved overmantel was installed in 1629, and probably the panelling too, and Henry's diary records his minute attention to the work of the joiners assembling it. The arms in the middle panel show those of Ferrers of Groby quartering Hampden (the family of Henry's grandmother).

Henry's diary for 1622, recalled: 'Besse warmed my bed and I went to it, and put on my cap warmed, and this nyght I lay in my bed in my new flannell wastecote all night and liked the making of it exceedingly well.... I said som[e] prayers after I was in bed, but being oppressed with sleepe I scarce tell how many I said, or whether I made an end of them as I should have don.'

The handsome carved and inlaid bed was made up from 17th-century fragments in the 19th century and collected for the house by Thomas Ferrers-Walker, whose bedroom this was. He may have chosen it for its pleasing view across the walled garden and towards the church.

Above A detail of the elaborate wooden chimneypiece (*c.*1629) in Henry Ferrers' Bedroom

Left A late 19th-century photograph showing Henry Ferrers' Bedroom with its elaborate heraldic carved wooden chimneypiece

The legend of Greycat

One of the animal inhabitants of Baddesley Clinton, who has become something of a legend, is Mr Ferrers-Walker's beloved Greycat, whose portrait hangs by the bed. There were three cats born in 1931, Greycat and his two sisters, Blackcat and Black-and-White Cat, but Greycat was special. Greycat always accompanied Mr Ferrers-Walker on walks, even as far as the church. He was so much a part of their life that Greycat appears in family portraits, and photographs of him can be seen throughout the house. Greycat died in 1952 and was buried under rhododendrons to the right of the house, facing the moat. When Mr Ferrers-Walker died in 1970, Greycat's head was engraved on his memorial.

The Blue Bedroom

The adjoining Blue Bedroom was once known as the White Bedroom, as the panelling had all been painted, probably in the 18th century. Thomas and Undine Ferrers-Walker removed layers of paint to reveal the original oak in the 1940s and in the 1950s hung the blue curtains from which this room takes its name.

The overmantel is thought to have been installed by Edward, son of Henry the Antiquary, as it includes his initials; the painted decoration was applied largely in the 19th century.

The handsome richly inlaid half-tester oak bed in this room was acquired by Lady Chatterton from an inn at Appledore in Kent, and the legend was that the wood had come from a Spanish galleon, one of the Armada fleet wrecked on the Kentish coast in 1588. This room was often used by the visiting priest responsible for saying Mass in the Chapel next door.

Above The Blue Bedroom bed is said to have been made from wood salvaged from a Spanish Armada galleon

Footsteps in the dark

The upper landing corridor, lined with family portraits, was originally an open-sided loggia. Rebecca Ferrers recalled that overnight guests reported hearing ghostly footsteps along the corridor at night and the door-handles of their room being tried. She had even heard it herself: 'I once heard that solemn tread. It had an indescribably awful and mournful sound, as of someone treading on one's heart and affected me deeply.' She added: 'It had a very weird effect to hear the handle jerked loudly within a few feet of where you are standing and see no one.' Rebecca identified the ghost as a Major Thomas Ferrers, who died in 1817, falling from the ramparts at Cambrai in France. She arranged a Mass to be said for his soul in 1877, after which the ghostly footsteps are said to have stopped.

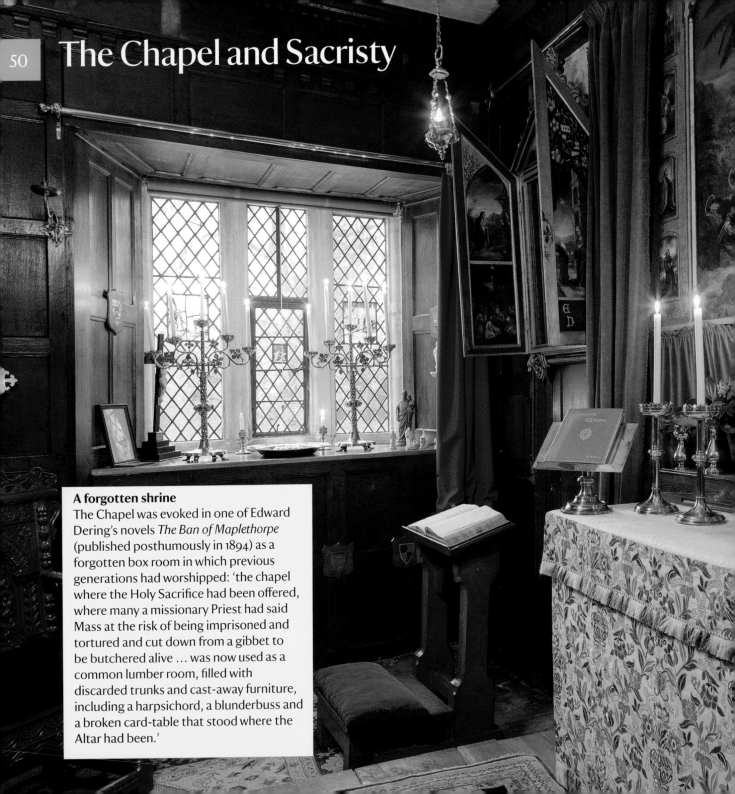

The Chapel and Sacristy

A forgotten shrine

The Chapel was evoked in one of Edward Dering's novels *The Ban of Maplethorpe* (published posthumously in 1894) as a forgotten box room in which previous generations had worshipped: 'the chapel where the Holy Sacrifice had been offered, where many a missionary Priest had said Mass at the risk of being imprisoned and tortured and cut down from a gibbet to be butchered alive … was now used as a common lumber room, filled with discarded trunks and cast-away furniture, including a harpsichord, a blunderbuss and a broken card-table that stood where the Altar had been.'

The Chapel at Baddesley Clinton lies in the oldest part of the house, where the private quarters of the lord of the manor were linked to the great chamber of the medieval house. As it has an access via the garderobe into the priest hole created by Nicholas Owen, it seems most likely that this room was used as a bedroom and chapel by the Jesuit priests who were sheltered here in the 1590s.

This room had long ceased to be used as a private place of worship when it was re-consecrated in 1875. The occasion was Lady Chatterton's second conversion, as she had been first received into the Catholic Church in 1865 by John Newman, but had clearly lapsed. There is a portrait of Newman, a friend and correspondent of the family, hanging on the landing. At first she wanted to build a whole new chapel in the courtyard (and even sketched the plan), but was persuaded that the revival of the old family chapel was a better plan.

The double door was fixed to the entrance of the current Sacristy at a later point, as in the medieval house this would have been an outside wall. This room was opened up in the 1940s by Thomas Ferrers-Walker, as part of his attempt to return the house to its 16th-century appearance. He removed partitions and even the 18th-century chimney from the Kitchen below to recapture this atmospheric space.

Left The Chapel by candlelight

Below The view into the Sacristy adjoining the Chapel

The Chapel reborn

In his *Memoirs of Georgiana, Lady Chatterton*, Edward Dering recorded the first time Mass was said here in 1875, 'after an interval of sixty years, by our kind friend, Monsignor Virtue.' He added: 'Lord Gainsborough was also staying with us at that time. As we were not yet provided with what was necessary, Monsignor Vertue brought with him a chalice, vestments, altar stone etc.'

Referring to the plan to build a chapel opposite the Gatehouse, he remarked: 'It would have been an act of Faith written in stone; but the restoration of the old chapel leaves a deeper mark. It is founded in the history of the past, hallowed by the former presence of martyrs and confessors, and it bridges the continuity of the Holy Sacrifice in an ancient Catholic house that never had an apostate owner.'

Articles of the faith

Rebecca certainly thought the presence of the carved angels in the 17th-century decoration of the room, which included the chimneypiece, proved that it had been a chapel. The reredos was painted by Rebecca, and depicts Christ in the Garden of Gethsemane flanked by representations of other saints.

The triptych to the left of the reredos of the Virgin Mary was painted by Lady Chatterton after an original painting by Sassoferrato which hung at Woburn Abbey. The small panels of scenes from the passion of Christ were painted by Rebecca, as was the Virgin and St John triptych, which appears on the right-hand side of the altar. The painted shields on the walls and ceiling were also painted by Rebecca and show the arms of the Ferrers and Dering family. The panels of antique Spanish leather were acquired for the Chapel by Lady Chatterton.

Above **Christ in the Garden of Gethsemane, painted by Rebecca, 1887**

Left **A candelabra and figurines on the windowsill in the Chapel**

Opposite top **Thomas Ferrers-Walker used old photographs of the Chapel to help him restore it in the 1940s**

Opposite below **The Virgin, triptych by Lady Chatterton, after Sassoferrato, *c.* 1870**

A new revival

In 1940 Thomas Ferrers-Walker re-created the Chapel as we see it now. It had ceased to be used after the death of Rebecca in 1923. One of her maidservants recalled how sad the house felt when the sanctuary lamp was extinguished in the Chapel where previously they had used to meet to say prayers every evening. Thomas Ferrers-Walker used early photographs which showed how the altar and paintings were placed and the Chapel was set out in the life of the Quartet; they suggest a chapel used as much for private devotion as for the celebration of Mass.

The Great Parlour

The Great Parlour over the Gatehouse is one of the finest rooms of the house and was the result of works by Edward Ferrers, son of Henry the Antiquary, after he inherited Baddesley in 1633. He created the barrel-vaulted ceiling – which he perhaps would have decorated with elaborate plasterwork had he had more funds – and added the mullioned and transomed window overlooking the moat. He also installed a handsomely carved heraldic overmantel, which was moved to the Great Hall in the 18th century.

Above The Great Parlour in 1897 when it was used by Rebecca as her studio

Below The Great Parlour was where more formal entertaining took place in the 1600s

Given this room's status, this was where honoured guests were entertained with the emphasis on dining, but such a room would also be used for musical entertainments and dancing. In the 16th century it was described as being hung with tapestry and was described as being similarly dressed in the 1890s – 'heavy folds of old tapestry cover the walls'. At this time the room was furnished with old oak as well as Chippendale, Boulle work and marquetry furniture.

The fine light from the great window meant that this room became in effect the painting room or studio for both Lady Chatterton and Rebecca.

A storm breaks

Rebecca recorded a dramatic scene in the Great Parlour in 1916. 'On the night of Monday March 29th and during all Tuesday a most terrifying storm of wind and snow – a blizzard such as had not occurred for 30 years or more swept over the midland counties…. An upper casement of the stone-mullioned high window facing east, of the banqueting room was blown in with the result that when the housemaid went into the room in the morning, she found the floor from end to end and all the furniture covered an inch deep with snow.'

The Library

The Library was adapted from a first-floor chamber on the north side of the courtyard. It was in this room that Henry the Antiquary thought Nicholas Brome murdered the priest who was flirting with his wife (see page 27). The dark stain on the floor has always been said to be a mark of the murder, although later analysis has shown it to be animal blood. What's more, family memoirs of the 1930s have revealed Cecil Ferrers, in a scene that could be lifted from P. G. Wodehouse, refreshing the blood to make the story more convincing to visitors!

In later centuries, this room was a bedroom, known as the Ghost Bedroom. It became a library in the 19th century, when it was used by the Quartet. The elegant carved overmantel was installed by Edward Ferrers and is dated 1634. Some of the books in the Library have been here since before the 1760 inventory, although Thomas Ferrers-Walker and his son collected many, with an emphasis on local history and genealogy. They also introduced the handsome oak lectern in the form of an eagle with outstretched wings, originally a ship's figurehead of around 1800.

Right The oak lectern in the form of an eagle made from a ship's figurehead

Preserving a very English jewel

Baddesley Clinton's historic atmosphere has been inspiring its owners and occupants with a devotion to its preservation that dates all the way back to the 17th century. This commitment to its care is as keen today, and we hope that you too have felt the special quality of this, the very model of a medieval moated manor house.

In 1978, the nation's leading country house expert John Cornforth wrote about the fragile and rare quality of Baddesley Clinton, lying only 14 miles from the centre of Birmingham. It was, he thought, 'a place to read about and ponder on, for it is the essence of a strand of English history that has become very rare. But that essence could be destroyed in half a day.'

The work of the National Trust at Baddesley Clinton to make sure this does not happen is supported by a large number of devoted and enthusiastic volunteers. These people endeavour to make that sense of love and warmth of welcome felt, the feelings that you can clearly discern not only in the diaries of 16th-century owner Henry Ferrers but also in the romantic lives of the Quartet in the 19th century.

Baddesley Clinton is of considerable historic interest, but it is also fascinating for the devotion it inspires in others, inspiration we hope you have also felt in the shadow of these ancient walls.

Above The preservation of Baddesley Clinton means it will continue to inspire visitors